To Brian
My amazing, remarkable son.
With much Love,

Mom

Christmas 2010

To My Amazing, Remarkable Son

Edited by
Douglas Pagels

Blue Mountain Press™
Boulder, Colorado

We gratefully acknowledge the permission granted by the following authors, publishers, and authors' representatives to reprint poems or excerpts from their publications: Susan Polis Schutz for "To My Son, with Love." Copyright © 1988 by Stephen Schutz and Susan Polis Schutz. Grand Central Publishing for "My son..." from PERMISSION SLIPS by Sherri Shepherd. Copyright © 2009 by Sherri Shepherd. Reprinted by permission of Grand Central Publishing. All rights reserved. And for "I send you off..." from LETTERS FROM DAD by John Broome with Jack Broome. Copyright © 1996 by John Broome. Reprinted by permission of Grand Central Publishing. All rights reserved. Cengage Learning, Inc., for "From the moment he was born..." by David Riley from THE FATHERS' BOOK: SHARED EXPERIENCES, edited by Carol Kort and Ronnie Friedland. Copyright © 1986 by Gale, a part of Cengage Learning, Inc. All rights reserved. Bantam Books, a division of Random House, Inc., for "From the very instant..." and "I stayed involved in..." from MOVING PICTURES: AN AUTOBIOGRAPHY by Ali MacGraw. Copyright © 1991 by Ali MacGraw. All rights reserved. Chaddock for "I don't remember how..." by Dargie Arwood and "There are lives I can imagine..." by Brian Andreas from SWINGS HANGING FROM EVERY TREE, edited and compiled by Ramona Cunningham. Copyright © 2001 by Dargie Arwood. All rights reserved. Crown Publishers, a division of Random House, Inc., for "Sometimes I see my son..." from AFTER THE FALL by Suzanne Somers. Copyright © 1998 by Suzanne Somers. All rights reserved. Stephen Koenig, MD for "Could it be that your choices now..." from "To Michael" from SACRED PROCESS by Karen Koenig. Copyright © 1993 by Karen Koenig. All rights reserved. Broadway Books, a division of Random House, Inc., for "I wanted him to know..." and "Everyone should have a moment..." from NO MOUNTAIN HIGH ENOUGH: RAISING LANCE, RAISING ME by Linda Armstrong Kelly. Copyright © 2005 by Linda Armstrong Kelly. All rights reserved. And for "One of the inspirations for 'Missing You'..." from MOSAIC: PIECES OF MY LIFE SO FAR by Amy Grant. Copyright © 2007 by Amy Grant. All rights reserved. Rachel Snyder for "Son." Copyright © 2007 by Rachel Snyder. All rights reserved. Lesley Ann Warren for "My child has always been..." from PORTRAITS OF LIFE by Joan Lauren. Copyright © 1994 by Lesley Ann Warren. All rights reserved. Bantam Books, a division of Random House, Inc., for "[My son] is the greatest thing that has ever..." from COMFORT FROM A COUNTRY QUILT by Reba McEntire. Copyright © 1999 by Reba McEntire. All rights reserved. Hazelden Foundation, Center City, MN, for "My son Colin was looking out..." from WRITING TO SAVE YOUR LIFE: HOW TO HONOR YOUR STORY THROUGH JOURNALISM by Michele Weldon. Copyright © 2001 by Hazelden Foundation. All rights reserved.

Acknowledgments are continued on the last page.

Library of Congress Control Number: 2010902791
ISBN: 978-1-59842-523-9

M and Blue Mountain Press are registered in U.S. Patent and Trademark Office.
Certain trademarks are used under license.

Printed in China.
First Printing: 2010

⊛ This book is printed on recycled paper.

This book is printed on paper that has been specially produced to be acid free (neutral pH) and contains no groundwood or unbleached pulp. It conforms with the requirements of the American National Standards Institute, Inc., so as to ensure that this book will last and be enjoyed by future generations.

Blue Mountain Arts, Inc.

P.O. Box 4549, Boulder, Colorado 80306

Contents

(Authors listed in order of first appearance)

To My Amazing, Remarkable Son

*E*ven after this book is read and set aside, I hope you will remember all the wishes and thoughts it holds inside...

Everywhere you journey in life, you will go with my love by your side.

Forever it will be with you: truly, joyfully, and more meant to be than words could ever say. You are the joy of my life, the source of my dearest memories, and the inspiration for my fondest wishes, and you are the sweetest present life could ever give to anyone.

I love you so much. I want you to remember that... every single day. And I want you to know that these are things I'll always hope and pray...

always,
Mom

That the world will treat you fairly. That people will appreciate the one-in-a-million person you are. That you will be safe and smart and sure to make good choices on your journey through life.

That a wealth of opportunities will come your way. That your blessings will be many, that your troubles will be few, and that life will be very generous in giving you all the happiness and success you deserve.

You're not just a fantastic son, you're a tremendous, rare, and extraordinary person. All the different facets of your life — the ones you reveal to the rest of the world and the ones known only to those you're close to — are so impressive. And as people look even deeper, I know they can't help but see how wonderful you are inside.

I'll always love you, Son, with all my heart. And I couldn't be more proud of you... if I tried.

— Douglas Pagels

My son... what would life be like without hearing your voice and seeing your smile? I first held you and wondered what the heck I'd signed up for. I hold you now and wonder why I waited so long for you. You are my everything.

You always have been - Mom

Sherri Shepherd

From the moment he was born, I was smitten with Jake, more, I think, than even my wife dared to hope. I never knew how much you could get by giving. Jake takes a lot of time, but he gives back a dimension to my life that I cherish....

There's a freshness about the way this little boy meets every morning that lifts up our lives. It's like the freshness of early morning sun sparkling off the dew on the grass. It's the same sun and same grass every morning, but it still makes your heart stop and take notice.

David Riley

Son, May These Words Always Remind You of My Love

One day you will want to know
that someone in this world
thinks the sun rises when you smile
and that nothing is as amazing as your laugh.
If ever you feel the burden of guilt or failure
    and believe that no one
could love you just the way you are,
    then remind yourself... I do.
I love you exactly as you are.

When I gave birth to you,
the miracle never left my heart
and changed me forever.
Every second you are with me
is a gift no one could ever
put a price on.
So remember...
you are the reason why
my life is so wonderful.

Forever in my heart, Mom

— Renate M. Braddy

The Universe Changes
When a Son Is Born

Last night my child was born — a very strong boy. If you ever become a father, I think the strangest and strongest sensation of your life will be hearing for the first time the thin cry of your own child. For a moment you have the strange feeling of being double; but there is something more... perhaps the echo in a woman's heart of all the sensations felt by all the fathers and mothers... at a similar instant in the past.

No man can possibly know what life means, what the world means, what anything means, until he has a child and loves it. Then the whole universe changes and nothing will ever again seem exactly as it seemed before.

Lafcadio Hearn

Nothing is ever the same.

Mom

From the very instant that I saw your big/little feet poking out from the basket in my room in the hospital... I have valued and respected and loved you unconditionally. With all of the fabulous adventures I have had in this first half of my life, it has been our friendship and trust that have been the biggest gift.

Ali MacGraw

yes . mom

I don't remember how I spent my time before loving this child. We thank God for him every day.

Dargie Arwood

mom

Son, I Want You to Know How Much You Mean to Me

Sometimes I can hardly believe
that the man I see when I look at you
used to be my little boy.
Where did the time go? *Yes, Where did the time go?*
How did the moments turn into years
that disappeared behind us
at such great speed?
I am in awe at the changes that
have taken place in you,
and sometimes it saddens me
because that part of my life is over.
Yet I also feel the happiness and pride
in having a son who is all grown up,
and nothing can dull or dampen
the wonderful memories I have
of you as my little boy.

*My boy who chopped
trees for dinner.*

Even the rough times, the trying times,
and the overwhelming times
have sweetened through the years.
Memories of you still bring
laughter and delight,
a warmness of heart,
and tears to my eyes.

The pride I have in you
and the love I feel for you
have continued to grow, much like you have.
You are even more precious to me now
than you were before.
If you could look inside my heart
and see the love there,
if you could feel its strength and depth,
then you would know that you
have fulfilled my life in ways
no other person ever could.

Barbara Cage

Brian

*S*ometimes I see ~~my~~ *you* son
And wish his mother had it all together
To give him strength and courage
   I only sometimes have
To listen when my own hurts need hearing
To hold him even though I am alone

But sometimes I see my son
With trust in his eyes no one else could give
With a smiling, shining face that says
   there was no failure
No monstrous mistakes
Only good things and memories of
   love and caring

Sometimes I see my son
And he touches me in secret corners
And I know everything is fine
And will always be

Suzanne Somers

So glad we all grew up.
Love Mom

Son.

I know your life is busy,
so I won't spend a lot of time
reminding you how much
I love you.
I'll just tuck all my hugs for you
inside this book.
I will fill it
with the pride I feel in you
and with a prayer
for all the things
that will make you happy,
help you stay healthy,
and keep you on the path
to your highest
and mightiest dreams.

 Jacqueline Schiff

Mom

Words to Help You
Be Strong
Along the Path of Life

I can barely begin to tell you of all my wishes for you ▪ There are so many of them, and I want them all to come true ▪ I want you to use your heart as a compass as you grow and find your way in the world, but I want you to always have an appreciation for the direction of home ▪ I want you to have self-esteem and self-confidence and to be self-sufficient but also to know that you will never be alone ▪ I want you to be safe and smart and cautious ▪ I want you to be wise beyond your years ▪ I don't want you to grow up too fast ▪ I want you to come to me with your fears ▪ I want the people who share your days to realize that they are in the presence of a very special someone ▪ You are a wonderful, rare person with no comparison ▪

I want you to know that opportunities will come, and you'll have many goals to achieve ▪ The more that obstacles get in the way of your dreams, the more you'll need to believe ▪ Get your feet wet with new experiences, but be sure you never get in over your head ▪ I want you to realize how capable you are and that your possibilities are unlimited ▪ I hope you never lose your childlike wonder, your delight and appreciation in interesting things ▪ I know you'll keep responding in a positive way to the challenges life always brings ▪ I want you to set the stage for living in a way that reflects good choices and a great attitude ▪ I want you to honor... the wonder of you ▪

▪ Douglas Pagels

mom

Could it be that your choices now
Are in some way a reflection
Of your positive feelings *Perhaps*
About how I did things
As you were growing up?
I hope so.

I always wish you the very best:
Deepest and highest blessings.
My heart goes with you
Always and ever,
Dear son. *The very best,*

Karen Koenig

Love mom

I wanted him to know he was the first and
best thing in my day. Every day.

Linda Armstrong Kelly

Everyday! Love mom

Son

Remember that rough-around-the-edges guy who used to stare back at you from the mirror? Take a fresh look, and maybe you'll see what the rest of us see. A young man with his feet on the ground and his eyes on the sky. A generous spirit and an open heart. And of course, that smile that just won't quit. Underneath it all, you have the courage to make your mark on the world in a way that is yours and yours alone.

Is it any wonder that the qualities that make you so very special are the same ones that make those who love you so very proud?

Never forget, Son, how amazing you are.

Rachel Snyder

So very proud,
Mom

My child has always been the light of my life. No matter what I was dealing with, my heart would always sing at the sound of his voice or the glimpse of his face.

Even when your voice changed & I didn't recognize it on the phone. Mom

■ Lesley Ann Warren

A good, praiseworthy son is the sun of his family.

yes

■ Hindu Proverb

[My son] is the greatest thing that has ever happened to me! He is the absolute highlight of my life.

He is my sunshine....

[He] is what unconditional love is all about.

■ Reba McEntire

My son Colin was looking out the window in the upstairs hallway in the muddled hours before school began one recent October morning. The sky was overcast and blue-gray — one of those mornings you wanted either to shrink back under the covers for escape or have a pot of strong, hot coffee brewing in order to make it through to 10:00 a.m. without yawning or trying repeatedly to skulk back to bed.

"It's a pretend sunny day," he surmised quickly. "It's sunny underneath."

Now here's a worldview I hope he takes with him through life. It sounds dangerously close to that pop-song, sunny-side approach, but I bet good money if he maintains that outlook, it will serve him well through high school, college, goodness knows through marriage and small children, even when his own children reach adolescence and they tell him he's wrong about everything and especially that attitude. I don't know for sure whether he gets this gregarious attitude from me, but I am definitely taking the credit.

Michele Weldon

It's Sunny underneath Always. Mom

A Mother Sees Her Son

Sometimes when I watched you climb a tree,
I didn't see the determination in your eyes —
Only your clumsiness and tattered shorts
    from the fall you shortly took.
I was thinking ruined shorts.
You were thinking mountains.

Sometimes when you took your bike and
    jumped your ramp in frolicsome danger,
I didn't see the bravery in your deed —
Only the foolhardy impending scar.
I was thinking emergency room.
You were thinking power and speed.

Sometimes when a grade was slipping
    and I feared failure,
I didn't see the other grades that were super —
Only the bad grade.
I was thinking it was my failure.
You were just thinking.

Some twenty years have come and gone,
And you have grown to be a young man.
I can see the power of your dreams,
    the height of your optimism, and
    the speed of your accomplishments.
Sometimes I just didn't see.

I always knew.
Mom

But I can now.

                Pat W. Stanley

*E*veryone should have a moment to believe
they're the center of someone's universe, and my
son and I gave that moment to each other. That's
what I want to tell people who ask me about
Lance: that he's my son... and I would think he
was the most amazing man in the world even
if the world had never heard his name. *Mom*

Watching him take his sport by storm (and
occasionally worrying about the sport taking
him), I'm continually astonished at the all-out
beauty of that boy and the enormous love he
brings out of me.

                Linda Armstrong Kelly

Beautiful Boy

Before you go to sleep
Say a little prayer
Every day in every way
It's getting better and better

Beautiful
Beautiful, beautiful
Beautiful boy

Out on the ocean sailing away
I can hardly wait
To see you come of age
But I guess we'll both
Just have to be patient
Yes it's a long way to go
A hard row to hoe
Yes it's a long way to go
But in the meantime

Before you cross the street
Take my hand
Life is just what happens to you
While you're busy making other plans

Beautiful
Beautiful, beautiful
Beautiful boy

John Lennon

*You were such a beautiful child
Everyone thought so
Especially me
Mom*

$\mathcal{A}$s a parent, I want to be a place you can come to... for shelter, for unconditional caring, for sharing all the support I can give. I want to be the person you can turn to... for answers and understanding or just to reinforce the feeling of how incredibly special you are.

Son, I want to do everything I possibly can for you... because that's what love does when it is strong and grateful and giving. I want you to know what a gift it is to be your dad and that my love for you is never-ending. *mom*

— Douglas Pagels

I love you
Mom

"I Have a Boy to Bring Up"

I have a boy to bring up. Help me to perform my task with wisdom, kindness, and good cheer. Help me always to see him clearly, as he is...

I have a boy to bring up. Give me great patience and a long memory. Let me remember the hard places of my own youth, so that I may help when I see him struggling as I struggled then. Let me remember the things that made me glad... lest I forget that a child's laughter is the light of life.

I have a boy to bring up. Teach me that love understands all things, knows no weakness, tolerates no selfishness.

I have a son to bring up... with the values of goodness and just rewards... and happiness.

Angelo Patri

Always happiness
from

Son, You're a Gift
I Appreciate So Much

You're light and laughter and a heart filled with promise. You're fun to be around. Few people are more caring, and you make me the luckiest parent of all.

When people like you grow up, it makes the whole world a better place. You're extraordinary in so many ways. I feel incredibly blessed to share life with you, and in my heart I'm about as proud as I can be.

You're everything any parent could ever wish for, and I can't imagine a more precious gift than you.

Every day of your life, may you experience all the joy you can feel, all the love you can hold, and all the dreams you can touch.

Even though you've heard this already, I want to say it again, you're special, Son, and I love you.

— Linda E. Knight

"*P*lease, God, don't let anything happen to my children." Bob offered up this simple prayer one September night in bed, as we have uttered it since the miracle of parenthood happened to us. It is a parent's deepest desire to be the human shield, the lightning rod, the four-leaf clover, and the lucky rabbit's foot. "Let me absorb all the pain for them," he says again, with an unwavering gaze at me. But we both know it doesn't work that way.

Not

Lee and Bob Woodruff

*A*s you grow and experience more things in your young life, know that there will inevitably be obstacles to encounter. But don't worry that they will seem too great for you to handle, because you can. You may doubt yourself at times, but know that if you have faith, you have everything. Faith is the key to being successful.

I knew you could

Mom

T. L. Nash

$\mathcal{A}$s parents we all have different ideas of what success means for our children. I think the most important aspect of success has to do with finding a real passion for something in life. It means a responsibility to live up to one's potential. That has to be discovered; it can't be forced upon a youngster growing up. We cannot expect children to be replicas of us. From the minute they emerge from the womb they are already themselves. That must be honored, and they must be given the tools and opportunities to go as far as they possibly can on their own.

Christopher Reeve

Hooray for Tools

Mom

A Note from "The Last Lecture"

*B*ecause I've been so vocal about the power of childhood dreams, some people have been asking lately about the dreams I have for my children.

I have a direct answer for that.

It can be a very disruptive thing for parents to have specific dreams for their kids. As a professor, I've seen many unhappy college freshmen picking majors that are all wrong for them. Their parents have put them on a train, and too often, judging by the crying during my office hours, the result is a train wreck.

As I see it, a parent's job is to encourage kids to develop a joy for life and a great urge to follow their dreams. The best we can do is to help them develop a personal set of tools for the task.

So my dreams for my kids are very exact: I want them to find their own path to fulfillment. And given that I won't be there, I want to make this clear: Kids, don't try to figure out what I wanted you to become. I want you to become what *you* want to become.

Randy Pausch

Thanks for sticking to your dreams

mom

To My Son, with Love

A mother tries to provide her son
with insight into the important things in life
in order to make his life
as happy and fulfilling as possible

A mother tries to teach her son
to be kind and generous toward other people
to be honest and forthright at all times
to be fair, treating men and women equally
to respect and learn from older people
to know himself well
to understand his strong and weak points
to accept criticism and learn from his mistakes
to have many interests to pursue
to have many goals to follow
to work hard to reach these goals

A mother tries to teach her son
to have a strong set of beliefs
to listen to his intelligence
to laugh and enjoy life
to appreciate the beauty of nature

A mother tries to teach her son
to express his feelings openly
    and honestly at all times
to realize that love is the best emotion
    that anyone can have
to value the family unit
    as the basis of stability

If I have provided you with an insight *some of*
into most of these things *Even some of*
then I have succeeded as a mother *these things*
in what I hoped to accomplish in raising you
If many of these things slipped by
while we were all so busy
I have a feeling that you know them anyway
And as your proud mother *Very proud*
I will always continue to love and support
everything you are and everything you do
I am always here for you, my son
I love you

— Susan Polis Schutz

*I do love you
with all my
heart. — mom*

$\mathcal{B}$eing a parent is both sublime and humbling. My child's joy in the moment, and the gift of his love, are teaching me the greatest lessons of my life.

Gates McFadden

$\mathcal{F}$rom the moment both of them entered my life, I knew I had done what God sent me to do. Everything else is just a bonus. We talk without speaking, support without request, listen to each other with our hearts. They have taught me more about life than I ever could have taught them.

Joe Sutton

You inspire and teach us, challenge us, and open our hearts daily, and we will be forever grateful.

Kenny and Julia Loggins

yes

Kids — more than anything else — need to know their parents love them.

Randy Pausch

Always know that I love you!

Every day, I tell them in some way or another that the world is a better place because you're in it!

Wynonna Judd

I think it whether or not I tell you out loud. I Love you! mom

You hope your children find their way. I've been lucky enough to find my way. And my hope is that they find that thing that allows them to feel good about themselves.

Kevin Costner

You are finding your way —

Whatever they do, I hope they do it well — and I hope they enjoy it. That's what's important to me.

Jack Nicklaus

Please enjoy.

I only hope I have been able to pass on to them what my parents gave me, the ability to believe in themselves and stand on their own. We stuck together, kids. We're the team; you're my star players!

Erin Brockovich

We can, when we stand up for what we know is right.

Love,
m

If my boys want to play basketball, that's fine. I'd rather they played another sport, but if that's what they want to do, then I'll support them. I'm never going to steer them away from something they want to do. I will try to give them as many options as possible. That's all I can do. They have to make their own decisions. But whatever they do, I'll support them....

I will always have a very open relationship with them and let them know that they can come and talk to me about anything. I want them to know that if I can help them get through anything that I will be there.

Michael Jordan

You will always
have my support -
no matter what your
decision is -

Mom

When my oldest son was playing football in high school and college, usually a day or two before his game I would call him from whatever city I was in for an NFL telecast. I would give him reminders about some physical aspects of the game — such as making sure he warmed up properly and that his drops were good and to use his snap count to try and draw the other team offside — and just talk about football in general.

"Remember, it's not always going to go well," I'd say. "There could be some bad times, and if you go through them, just forget them — move on and remain positive. Whatever happens in your mind, your body will respond accordingly. If you think positive, your body will react that way, too." I'd like to take full credit for those words, but I can't. Bill Parcells said them to me any number of times. Good advice is worth passing along.

Think positively

■ Phil Simms

I would love my children to understand that if you live your life as honestly and ethically as possible, you'll never have to compromise your values.

■ Greg LeMond

I want my son to be a man of good heart who reaches out to the world around him with an open mind and a gentle touch.

■ Kent Nerburn

I have nothing more at heart, my dear son, than your success.

■ Daniel Webster

Wishes for a Wonderful Son

Son, may you find happiness in every direction your paths take you. May you never lose that sense of wonder you have always had, and may you hold on to the sense of humor you use to brighten the lives of everyone who knows you. May you go beyond the ordinary steps and discover extraordinary results. May you keep on trying to reach for your stars, and may you never forget how wonderful you are.

May you meet every challenge you are faced with, recognize every precious opportunity, and be blessed with the knowledge that you have the ability to make every day special.

May you have enough material wealth to meet your needs, while never forgetting that the real treasures of life are the loved ones and friends who are invaluable to the end. May you search for serenity and discover it was within you all along.

May you be strong enough to keep your hopes and dreams alive. May you always be gentle enough to understand. May you know that you hold tomorrow within your hands and that the way there will be shared with the makings of what will be your most wonderful memories. And may you always remember, each step of the way...

You are loved, Son, more than words can ever begin to say.

— Douglas Pagels

You are loved, son —
more than words —
To the moon & back
many times —
mom

Children are so rewarding. To have kids, that makes it easy to get through any problem. I find myself looking at my children, just watching them and realizing how fortunate I am. Everything I've done on the basketball court, in business, nothing compares to having them. And I'm sure other people feel the same way about their kids.

Family provides a foundation like nothing else can.

■ Michael Jordan

You hope that you give them a strong foundation — and that we never ever lose touch with who really gives support and where the real meaning of life comes from — your family.

■ Joe Montana

I think you can find pleasure in your work, but the things that are truly joyful, joy-producing, well, these are all about your family and friends.

■ Tom Hanks

I used to define myself by what happened in my career. I now define myself by what happens when I walk into the apartment at night.

Maybe it's different for other people, but for me being a parent is so far beyond what I imagined that it's hard to believe....

Once a week, rain or shine, I have lunch with Jack, just the two of us. Usually I take him downstairs to the Rock Center Café. I am never in a better mood than after I have talked to him for an hour... conversing with him is the best part of my week.

■ Matt Lauer

Home Is Where the Heart Is

We live in a single-story two-bedroom house with weathered gray siding and a rust-colored roof. When we learned two babies were coming, one of the first things Tom said was, "We'll have to put an addition on the house. We'll need more room." He said this with an air of resignation, because we didn't have the money for more babies, or more house. I reassured him babies don't take up much space, at least at first, and that a new coat of paint on the old bedroom would be fine.

Because it was the request of a terribly pregnant woman, or because it was simply cheaper, we replaced talk of the addition with talk of paint color. We decided on a functional, if bland, off-white. Tom would do the painting, as I needed to stay away from the fumes. Carter could help. We opened all the windows and set up box fans, and the two men in my life, big and small, worked on the room.

I'd sneak in and scribble words on the walls yet to be painted, things like "happiness" and "laughter" and "love," Carter's eyes growing big because I was writing on the walls. "It's okay, honey," I said. "We'll cover it all up, but it will still be there, like a secret, or a wish. For good things, for all of us." Tom was reluctant at first, but he got into the spirit and added "music" and "books." Carter asked that we write "sunshine" and "chocolate milk."

Jennifer Graf Groneberg

The family is one of nature's masterpieces.

George Santayana

Would that it
Could have been —
So glad you have
the family now, that
you always wanted —
love,
mom

The best thing about being a father is when you get feedback from the kids — smiles on their faces. That's the stuff that I love.

Doug Flutie

There are lives I can imagine without children, but none of them have the same laughter and noise.

Brian Andreas

Families have more to do with common memories than common genes. They're more about sharing experiences than sharing blue eyes or curly hair.

Anne Hillerman

Thoughts from the Parents
of Adopted Children

*M*arie and I hereby submit our answer to the universal question of those considering adoption. The question concerns parental love for kids you haven't produced yourselves. The answer is don't worry about it. As veterans of raising both kinds we can testify that all of them provoke affection, irritation, worry, joy, dismay, care, pride, anger, and, most of all, love. Each and every one of them is our child.

Tony Hillerman

*M*y children... make fatherhood a blessing, a joy, and a wonderful challenge each and every day.

Al Roker

and Oh, Brian! coming from the chippies in the front row.

I made it a point not to push any of my kids into football, though since he likes it I help him, just as my dad helped me. Michael also likes to play music. Especially rap music. And so in some respects I've discovered what my parents must have gone through at times with me. You need patience. Understanding. And, occasionally, ear plugs.

I remember your band in school and you singing

▦ Dan Marino

I stayed involved in my son's activities, in and out of school. There was always something very reassuring to me about the day-to-day minutiae of soccer games and school projects, parent meetings and birthday parties. I devoted a lot of time to these everyday involvements, grateful for the opportunity to be an active part of my son's childhood and development.

Sorry to have missed this part.

▦ Ali MacGraw

Notes from a
Class Field Trip

*W*hen... we all eat lunch in a park, I watch these boys interact with their mothers....

For a few minutes, these boys are just that — little boys — clamoring for their mothers. I feel a stab of sentiment and find my eyes blurring with tears as I watch this interplay, but I don't want to blink them away. I am afraid to miss any part of this brief time in Blaze's childhood and I believe a blink is as long as it will take for Blaze and the rest of those boys to cross over from being the children they are to the adolescents they are becoming.

■ Debra Ginsberg

Watching you
Climb confidently to
the top of the jungle
gym was delightful !
I knew you could.
Mom

Through the Open Door: Thoughts on What Lies Ahead and What Stays Behind

There is always one moment in childhood when the door opens and lets the future in.

watching with you write with both hands as your colorful artwork made me know about you —

Graham Greene

There are so many new horizons ahead. In the blink of an eye, sons are out the door and off to college, off to jobs, and eventually on to setting up their own homes and tending to their families and future lives. It's a time when parents hope and pray that all the values and lessons they tried to instill will help to light the way for the journey ahead.

May that light Shine on you forever.

Mom

And I am no exception: I want great things *Always* for you, too... and I have an enormous amount of faith in your ability to make your life a happy one. You take with you, everywhere you go, a supply of confidence, common sense, ability, determination, understanding, wisdom, and so many attributes that just sparkle inside you. You know how to make the right choices, and I know that you will.

But of all the things you take with you, you should know that you also leave something behind. Some people call it an "empty nest," but in its own special way, there's nothing empty about it. It will always be abundantly filled with wishes, support, hugs and hopes, an open line of communication, a close and caring bond, a sense of belonging, and a strong and constant love.

⬛ Douglas Pagels

Mom

Your bright smiles and warm hugs at the end of the day make it all worthwhile, and we love you, whether we're with you or apart.

Kenny and Julia Loggins

My dearest [son]...

I am longing to see you. I am sure there are many more things, which I shall remember as soon as this is posted, that I wished to say. But what I personally need, probably more than anything, is two or three days consultation and interchange with *you*... I now regret daily that we are separated by a distance too great.

J. R. R. Tolkien

Perhaps not so
great a distance
As I know, we
have time.
Mom

Words to My Son, During a Difficult Time

He said he never forgot a conversation I had with him... I assured him of our love, no matter what he did, where he went, or how he ended up. He knew that he could always phone us, collect, from anywhere in the world, and that whenever he wanted to come home, the door would always be open. He also knew we would never stop praying for him.

Billy Graham

Having someplace to go is home.
Having someone to love is family.
Having both is a blessing.

Anonymous

Such a blessing

mom

One of the inspirations for "Missing You" came from my sister Mimi's experience of sending her oldest son, my nephew Logan, to college....

One morning in late October, she was standing in my kitchen having a cup of coffee. Out of the blue and quite nonchalantly, Mimi mentioned that she'd bought a longer cord for her bedroom telephone. (These were before pocket-sized cell-phone days.)

"That way if I'm taking a bath, I can pull the phone all the way to the tub. I'd hate to miss his call," she said.

That one comment spoke volumes.

■ Amy Grant

I love cell phones

mom

Missing You

Your smile lights up a room
Like a candle in the dark
Warms me through and through
And I guess that I had dreamed
We would never be apart
But that dream did not come true

And missing you is just a part of living
Missing you feels like a way of life
I'm living out the life that I've been given
But baby I still wish you were mine

I cannot hear the telephone
Jangle on the wall
And not feel a hopeful thrill
And I cannot help but smile
At any news of you at all
I guess I always will

Amy Grant

*I missed you
every day in
still do —
Mom*

I send you off... with the joy of a father who has tried his best to provide his son with a solid foundation for his life and has seen his son thrive under every challenge and opportunity.

I love you... I'm behind you all the way.

I am always behind you — perhaps now beside you — Love, mom

■ John Broome

*Y*ou have grown into a young man whose insight, compassion, and thoughtfulness reflect in everything you do. They touch everyone who is fortunate enough to know you.

Through the years, our lives change — we grow, learn, and expand. But one thing remains the same in this mother's soul: the little boy who stole my heart the day he was born is the man who makes me beam with pride today.

■ Kathryn Leibovich

mom

Sometimes we need reminders in our lives of how much people care. If you ever get that feeling, I want you to remember this...

I love you, Son. Beyond any words that can even begin to tell you how much...

I hold you and your happiness within my heart each and every day. I am so proud of you and so thankful to the years that have given me so much to be thankful for.

If I were given a chance to be anything I wanted to become, there's nothing I would rather be than your parent.

And there is no one I'd rather have... as my son.

— Douglas Pagels

Acknowledgments continued…

We gratefully acknowledge the permission granted by the following authors, publishers, and authors' representative to reprint poems or excerpts from their publications: Pat W. Stanley for "A Mother Sees Her Son." Copyright © 20 by Pat W. Stanley. All rights reserved. Lenono Music for "Beautiful Boy" written by John Lennon. Copyright © 19 by Lenono Music. Reprinted by permission. All rights reserved. Random House, Inc., for "'Please, God, don't let anything…" from IN AN INSTANT: A FAMILY'S JOURNEY OF LOVE AND HEALING by Lee and Bob Wood Copyright © 2007 by Lee Woodruff and Bob Woodruff. All rights reserved. And for "As parents we all have differe ideas…" from NOTHING IS IMPOSSIBLE: REFLECTIONS ON A NEW LIFE by Christopher Reeve. Copyrigh 2002 by Cambria Productions, Inc. All rights reserved. Hyperion for "Because I've been so vocal…" and "Kids — than anything else…" from THE LAST LECTURE by Randy Pausch. Copyright © 2008 by Randy Pausch. Reprin by permission. All rights reserved. And for "I used to define myself…" by Matt Lauer and "My children…" by Al Roker from BIG SHOES by Al Roker and Friends. Copyright © 2005 by Al Roker. Reprinted by permission. All ri reserved. Gates McFadden for "Being a parent is both sublime and humbling" from PORTRAITS OF LIFE by Joa Lauren. Copyright © 1994 by Gates McFadden. All rights reserved. Joe Sutton for "From the moment both of them entered…" from FATHER & SON: THE BOND by Bill Hanson. Copyright © 1996 by Joe Sutton. All rights reserve HarperCollins Publishers for "You inspire and teach us…" and "Your bright smiles…" from THE UNIMAGINAB LIFE by Kenny and Julia Loggins. Copyright © 1997 by Kenny and Julia Loggins. All rights reserved. And for "If my boys want to play…" and "Children are so rewarding" from MORE RARE AIR: I'M BACK by Michael Jorda Copyright © 1995 by Rare Air, Ltd. Text © 1995 by Michael Jordan. All rights reserved. And for "When my oldest son…" from SUNDAY MORNING QUARTERBACK by Phil Simms and Vic Carucci. Copyright © 2004 by Phil Simms and Vic Carucci. All rights reserved. And for "I would love my children…" by Greg LeMond, "You hope th you give them…" by Joe Montana, and "The best thing about…" by Doug Flutie from HE'S JUST MY DAD! by Diane Long. Copyright © 2000 by Diane Long. Foreword copyright © 2000 by John Grisham. All rights reserved. And for "Marie and I hereby submit…" by Tony Hillerman and "Families have more to do…" by Anne Hillerman from SELDOM DISAPPOINTED by Tony Hillerman. Copyright © 2001 by Tony Hillerman. All rights reserved. A for "When… we all eat lunch…" from RAISING BLAZE by Debra Ginsberg. Copyright © 2002 by Debra Ginsbe All rights reserved. And for "He said he never forgot…" from JUST AS I AM by Billy Graham. Copyright © 1997 Billy Graham Evangelistic Association. All rights reserved. Dutton Signet, a division of Penguin Group (USA), Inc "Every day, I tell them…" from COMING HOME TO MYSELF by Wynonna Judd. Copyright © 2005 by Wynon Judd. All rights reserved. And for "We live in a single-story…" from ROAD MAP TO HOLLAND by Jennifer Gra Groneberg. Copyright © 2008 by Jennifer Graf Groneberg. All rights reserved. William Morris Endeavor Entertain LLC, on behalf of Kevin Costner, for "You hope your children find…" from "Kevin Can Wait" by Fred Schruers (A July & August 2007). Copyright © 2007 by Kevin Costner. All rights reserved. New World Library, Novato, CA, w newworldlibrary.com, for "I want my son to be…" from LETTERS TO MY SON by Kent Nerburn. Copyright © 1999 by Kent Nerburn. All rights reserved. William Morris Endeavor Entertainment, LLC, on behalf of Erin Brock for "I only hope I have…" from TAKE IT FROM ME by Erin Brockovich. Copyright © 2002 by Erin Brockovich. All rights reserved. Courage Books, an imprint of Running Press, for "Whatever they do…" by Jack Nicklaus from FATHERS AND SONS by Todd Richissin. Text copyright © 2000 by Todd Richissin. All rights reserved. Meredith Corporation for "I think you can find pleasure…" by Tom Hanks from "Why We Love Tom Hanks" by Molly Hask (Ladies' Home Journal: April 2001). Copyright © 2001 by Meredith Corporation. All rights reserved. Triumph Boo for "I made it a point not…" from MY LIFE IN FOOTBALL by Dan Marino. Copyright © 2005 by Dan Marino. A rights reserved. Viking Penguin, a division of Penguin Group (USA), Inc., for "There is always one moment…" fro THE POWER AND THE GLORY by Graham Greene. Copyright © 1940, renewed © 1968 by Graham Greene. All r reserved. Houghton Mifflin Harcourt Publishing Company for "My dearest [son]…" by J. R. R. Tolkien from THE LETTERS OF J. R. R. Tolkien, edited by Humphrey Carpenter with the assistance of Christopher Tolkien. Copyrig 1981 by George Allen & Unwin [Publishers] Ltd. Reprinted by permission. All rights reserved. Age to Age Music, for "Missing You" by Amy Grant. Copyright © 1997 Age to Age Music, Inc./Warner Chappell. All rights reserved.

A careful effort has been made to trace the ownership of selections used in this anthology in order to obtain permission to reprint copyrighted material and give proper credit to the copyright owners. If any error or omi has occurred, it is completely inadvertent, and we would like to make corrections in future editions provided written notification is made to the publisher:

BLUE MOUNTAIN ARTS, INC., P.O. Box 4549, Boulder, Colorado 80306.

I used many
kleenex's to get through
this little book. It took
so sitting to read it in comment
to the end. The tears & memories
were many —
Suffice it to say — I love you.
Always have and always will, no
matter what —

Your Mother —

Charlotte
2010